The Pioneer Woman New Cookbook

120+ Simple And Delicious Recipes Will Make You Intelligent And Healthy Day By Day

By

Jennifer R. Turpin

PUBLISHED BY: *Jennifer R. Turpin*

Contents:

Introduction

n the distant past, in a galaxy far, far away...

I hosted a competition/giveaway in the spring of 2008, where participants had to submit one of their favorite recipes. By the time the day was up, the comments section was filled to the brim, and I think a mixer was the winner. These were the recipes that the contestants prepared most frequently and were their favorites. Being able to access such a reward was quite thrilling.

I went through pages and pages of the recipes after the contest was over, hoping there was a way to classify them and make them searchable. Naturally, this gave me the idea that was so obvious: I needed a recipe site—a fun, attractive one, where parents, single people, foodies, freaks, dweebs, and friends could gather and exchange the greatest recipes they had. I'm done now! I reminded myself. recipe websites

I then turned to look at my mound of laundry and started to sob.

In fact, I sobbed nonstop for the whole year and then some.

A recipe website for you, your mother, your boyfriend, and your friend is called Tasty Kitchen. It's for common bloggers, food bloggers, and pals who are Romans or from the same country. even accountants and Mary Kay consultants! I can't wait to look through the user profiles, recipe ratings, recipe reviews, and other fun content, as well as try the recipes.

When it comes to food bloggers: I built Tasty Kitchen because I wanted food bloggers to be able to publish recipes from their own websites and link back to those recipe postings from their Tasty Kitchen dishes. The same goes for "typical" (read: "ordinary") bloggers! There are many options to discover new, interesting websites to read, as member profiles allow you to insert your own website URL.

Since Tasty Kitchen is very new, there may be a few glitches here and there, but rest assured that it will continue to improve. And it's easy; I wanted it to be simple. In the upcoming weeks, I'll be adding some amazing features, but I didn't want to overwhelm it with options and connections.

Last but not least, despite my one-woman ineptitude, I want to thank Windows for helping me launch Tasty Kitchen. They didn't force me to promise them my fifth kid (no, I'm not pregnant...I think), demand that I accept money or valuables in exchange for my services, or require that I sign anything with my salty perspiration. They went above and above to help me create Tasty Kitchen because it wasn't an easy undertaking. On my own, I couldn't have completed the task. Windows has made it possible for Windows Live IDs to be integrated into Tasty Kitchen, allowing users who already have Live IDs (as well as Hotmail or MSN Messenger accounts) to sign in with those accounts.

I believe that I adore Windows.

Recipes

GREEK 7-LAYER DIP

Ingredients:

- 1 can (15 oz) chickpeas, drained and rinsed
- 1/2 cup chopped fresh parsley
- 1/2 cup chopped fresh mint
- 1/4 cup chopped fresh dill
- 1/4 cup chopped fresh cilantro
- 1/4 cup olive oil
- 3 cloves garlic, minced
- 1 teaspoon kosher salt
- 1/2 teaspoon black pepper

Instructions:

1. Preheat the oven to 350°F (175°C).

2. Spread the chickpea mixture in an 8x8 inch baking dish.

3. In a small bowl, whisk together the parsley, mint, dill, cilantro, olive oil, garlic, salt and pepper. Pour over the chickpea mixture and spread evenly.

4. Bake for 20 minutes or until heated through. Serve warm or at room temperature.

FESTIVE BRIE BITES

Ingredients:

- 8 ounces brie cheese
- 1 teaspoon dried thyme
- 1/2 teaspoon garlic powder
- 1/4 teaspoon paprika
- 1/4 teaspoon salt
- 1/8 teaspoon black pepper
- 8 thin slices crusty bread
- 1 large egg, beaten
- 1 tablespoon olive oil

Instructions:

1. Preheat oven to 350 degrees F. Line a baking sheet with parchment paper. In a small bowl, combine thyme, garlic powder, paprika, salt and pepper. Sprinkle mixture over each slice of bread.
2. Divide cheese evenly among the slices. On a low speed setting, beat egg in a medium bowl. Pour egg mixture over cheese on the bread slices.
3. Top each with one slice of bread. Press down gently to help the egg mixture adhere.
4. Place on prepared baking sheet and bake for 10 minutes or until golden brown. If desired, broil for 1 minute or until cheese is melted and bubbly.
5. Drizzle with olive oil before serving

BAKED BRIE WITH MUSHROOMS

Ingredients:

- 8 oz. brie cheese
- 8 oz. mushrooms, sliced
- 1 tbsp. olive oil
- salt and pepper to taste

Instructions:

1. Preheat oven to 375 degrees F. Grease a baking dish with olive oil and place the sliced mushrooms on top.
2. Sprinkle salt and pepper on top of the mushrooms.
3. Place the brie cheese on top of the mushrooms and bake for about 20 minutes, or until the cheese is melted and bubbly.
4. Enjoy!

BAKED WINGS WITH HABANERO HONEY

Ingredients:

- 6-8 chicken wings (you will need about 2 cups of wing meat)
- 1/2 cup Habanero Honey
- 1/4 cup soy sauce
- 1 tablespoon garlic powder
- 1 teaspoon onion powder
- 1/2 teaspoon black pepper

Instructions:

1. Preheat oven to 375 degrees F. In a small bowl, combine soy sauce, garlic powder, onion powder, and black pepper.
2. Place the wings in a baking dish and pour the soy sauce mixture over them. Bake for 25 minutes or until cooked through.
3. Serve hot with your favorite dipping sauce.

FRIED PASTA CHIPS

Ingredients:

- 1 pound spaghetti
- 1/2 cup canola oil
- 1/4 cup all-purpose flour
- 1 teaspoon garlic powder
- Salt and pepper, to taste

Instructions:

1. Cook the spaghetti according to package instructions.

2. While the spaghetti is cooking, heat the oil in a large skillet over medium heat.

3. Add the flour and garlic powder to the hot oil and stir until combined.

4. Add salt and pepper, to taste, and allow the mixture to cook for 1 minute.

5. Drain the cooked spaghetti and add it to the skillet with the sauce. Mix well and serve warm or cold.

STEPPED-UP SAUSAGE BALLS

Ingredients:

- 1 pound sausage
- 1/2 cup bread crumbs
- 1/4 cup grated Parmesan cheese
- 1 teaspoon garlic powder
- 1/4 teaspoon onion powder
- 1 tablespoon olive oil
- 2 tablespoons water

Instructions:

1. Preheat oven to 375 degrees Fahrenheit.

2. In a bowl, mix together the bread crumbs, Parmesan cheese, garlic powder and onion powder.

3. Add the sausage to the bowl, and mix until well combined.

4. Shape mixture into 1 inch balls and place on a baking sheet lined with parchment paper.

5. Bake in preheated oven for 15 minutes, or until slightly browned.

6. Remove from oven and drizzle with olive oil and water. Serve immediately

CHOCOLATE CHIP SCONES

Ingredients:

- 1/2 cup (1 stick) unsalted butter, at room temperature
- 2 cups all-purpose flour
- 1 teaspoon baking powder
- 1/4 teaspoon baking soda
- 1/2 teaspoon salt
- 3/4 cup sugar
- 2 large eggs, beaten
- 2 tablespoons milk
- 1 1/2 cups semisweet chocolate chips

Instructions:

1. Preheat oven to 400 degrees F (200 degrees C). Line a baking sheet with parchment paper.

2. In the bowl of an electric mixer fitted with the paddle attachment, beat the butter on medium speed until smooth. Add the flour, baking powder, baking soda and salt and mix until just combined.

3. Add the sugar and eggs and mix until well combined.

4. Reduce the mixer speed to low and add the milk. Mix just until combined.

5. Stir in the chocolate chips and mix until evenly distributed.

6. Drop dough by rounded tablespoons onto the prepared baking sheet. Bake for 12 to 15 minutes, or until golden brown and cooked through.

PINEAPPLE SMOOTHIE BOWLS

Ingredients:

- 1 cup pineapple
- 1 banana
- 2 cups almond milk
- 1 tbsp honey or maple syrup
- handful of ice cubes

Instructions:

1) Add all ingredients to a blender and blend until smooth.

2) Pour mixture into bowls and enjoy!

BREAD OMELET

Ingredients:

- One loaf of bread
- Eggs
- Garlic cloves
- Onion
- Green bell pepper
- Tomato sauce
- Salt and pepper to taste

Instructions:

1. Slice the bread into thin pieces.

2. In a large skillet, scramble eggs and add garlic, onion, bell pepper, tomato sauce, salt and pepper.

3. Add the bread slices and let them cook until they are browned on both sides.

4. Serve with your favorite potatoes or vegetable.

FRUITY BREAKFAST GALETTE

Ingredients:

- 1 puff pastry sheet
- 1 egg
- 1/4 cup diced strawberries
- 1/4 cup diced grapefruit
- 1/4 cup diced pineapple
- 1 tablespoon sugar
- Pinch of salt

Instructions:

1. Preheat oven to 400 degrees F.

2. On a lightly floured surface, roll pastry dough to 1/8-in.-thickness. Cut into 12 wedges. Line a baking sheet with parchment paper.

3. Whisk together egg, strawberries, grapefruit, pineapple and sugar in a small bowl; season with salt. Place half of the fruit mixture on each wedge of dough. Fold the bottom over the filling, then press down to seal. Trim any excess dough from around edges of galettes. Bake for 20 minutes or until golden brown.

MEXICAN FRITTATA

Ingredients:

- 1 diced onion
- 1 diced green pepper
- 1 diced red pepper
- 1 can black beans, rinsed and drained
- 1 can corn, rinsed and drained
- 2 eggs
- 1 tablespoon olive oil or vegetable oil
- Salt and pepper to taste

Instructions:

1. Preheat the oven to 400 degrees F (200 degrees C).
2. In a large bowl, mix together the onions, peppers, black beans, corn, eggs, and olive oil.
3. Season with salt and pepper to taste.
4. Pour the mixture into an 8x8 inch baking dish.
5. Bake for 15 minutes or until golden brown.

LEFTOVER FRITTATA SANDWICH

Ingredients:

- 1/2 cup leftover cooked frittata
- 1 slice of ham
- 1 slice of cheese
- 1 piece of bread
- 1 tablespoon olive oil
- Sea salt and black pepper to taste

Instructions:

1. Preheat the oven to 350 degrees Fahrenheit.

2. Spread the frittata on one slice of bread.

3. Sprinkle with cheese, ham, and a pinch of salt and pepper.

4. Heat olive oil in a pan over medium heat and cook the sandwich until the cheese is melted and bubbly.

5. Slice in half and serve warm!

THE ENGLISH BREAKFAST SITUATION

Ingredients:

- 1 cup of strong coffee
- 2 eggs
- 1 slice of toast
- 1 teaspoon of sugar
- A pinch of salt
- A smear of butter or margarine

Instructions:

1. Preheat the oven to 160 degrees Celsius (320 degrees Fahrenheit).

2. Beat the eggs in a bowl.

3. Melt the butter or margarine in a frying pan over a low heat.

4. Pour the eggs into the pan, stirring constantly with a wooden spoon until they are cooked and set.

5. Pour the coffee into a mug and stir in the sugar and salt.

6. Place the toast on a serving dish and top with the egg mixture. Serve immediately.

SHEET PAN PANCAKES

Ingredients:

- 1 cup all-purpose flour
- 1 teaspoon baking powder
- 1/2 teaspoon baking soda
- pinch of salt
- 1/4 cup sugar
- 2 tablespoons butter, melted
- 1 large egg
- 1/4 cup milk
- 1 tablespoon honey

Instructions:

1. Preheat oven to 400 degrees F (200 degrees C). Grease a 9x13 inch baking dish with butter.

2. In a medium bowl, whisk together the flour, baking powder, baking soda and salt.

3. In another medium bowl, whisk together the sugar, butter and egg until well combined. Add the wet ingredients to the dry ingredients and mix until just combined. Do not overmix.

4. Pour batter into the prepared baking dish and bake for 25 minutes or until golden brown and a toothpick inserted into the center comes out clean. Serve hot.

CRUNCHY BREAKFAST WRAPS

Ingredients:

- 8-10 slices of Ezekiel bread
- 1-2 tablespoons olive oil or butter
- 4 eggs
- 1 cup of shredded cheese
- salt and pepper to taste

Instructions:

1. Heat the olive oil or butter in a large skillet over medium heat.

2. Beat the eggs in a bowl.

3. Spread a layer of egg on each slice of Ezekiel bread.

4. Sprinkle with cheese, salt and pepper, and repeat layering until all ingredients are used up.

5. Place the skillet in the oven and bake for 8-10 minutes, until the egg is cooked through and the toast is golden brown and crispy. Serve immediately.

BUTTER PECAN FRENCH TOAST

Ingredients:

- 1 loaf of bread
- Butter
- Pecan halves
- Eggs
- Maple syrup
- Blueberries

Instructions:

1. Preheat your oven to 350 degrees Fahrenheit.

2. Cut your bread into 1 inch slices and spread butter on each slice.

3. Place the slices in a baking dish and bake for about 10 minutes, or until golden brown and crispy.

4. Meanwhile, whisk together eggs and maple syrup in a small bowl.

5. Once the bread is crispy, top with blueberries and egg mixture. Serve hot!

BREAKFAST GRILLED CHEESE

Ingredients:

- 1-2 slices of bread
- grated cheese
- butter or margarine
- chopped green onions (optional)

Instructions:

1. Preheat your grill to medium-high heat.

2. Spread butter or margarine on one slice of bread.

3. Top with cheese and another slice of bread, buttered side down.

4. Close grill lid and cook for about 3 minutes, or until bread is toasted and cheese is melted.

5. Remove from grill and top with chopped green onions, if desired.

Ingredients:

- 1/2 cup all-purpose flour
- 1/4 teaspoon baking powder
- pinch of salt
- 1/4 cup sugar
- 1 tablespoon unsalted butter, melted
- 1 egg
- 1/2 cup white chocolate chips
- 1/2 cup blueberries

Instructions:

1. Preheat oven to 350 degrees F (175 degrees C). Grease a baking sheet.

2. In a medium bowl, whisk together flour, baking powder and salt. In a small bowl, whisk together sugar and butter. Make a well in the center of the flour mixture and pour in sugar mixture and egg. Stir until ingredients are just combined. Stir in white chocolate chips and blueberries.

3. Drop batter by rounded tablespoons onto prepared baking sheet. Bake for 12 to 14 minutes, or until golden brown and cooked through. Serve immediately.

BAKED BAGEL EGG-IN-THE-HOLES

Ingredients:

- 2 bagels
- 1/2 tablespoon olive oil
- 1/4 teaspoon salt
- 1/4 teaspoon black pepper
- 8 eggs
- 2 tablespoons prepared horseradish, divided

Instructions:

1. Preheat oven to 400 degrees F (200 degrees C). Cut bagels in half and brush both sides with olive oil.
2. Sprinkle each half with salt and black pepper.
3. Place egg-in-the-holes on the cut bagels, dividing evenly.
4. Drizzle 1 tablespoon horseradish over each egg-in-the-hole.
5. Bake for 17 minutes or until golden brown.

DALTON COFFEE

Ingredients:

- 1 cup of Dalton coffee
- 1/2 teaspoon of sugar
- 1 teaspoon of vanilla extract
- 1 egg
- 1 tablespoon of melted butter
- 1 cup of all-purpose flour
- 1/4 teaspoon of baking powder
- 1/4 teaspoon of salt

Instructions:

1. Preheat the oven to 350 degrees Fahrenheit. Grease a 9x13 inch baking dish.

2. In a medium bowl, combine the coffee, sugar, and vanilla extract. Beat the egg until it is light and fluffy. Stir in the melted butter. Add the flour, baking powder, and salt; mix well. Pour the batter into the baking dish.

3. Bake for 25 minutes or until golden brown and set. Let cool before serving.

MUG OMELETS

Ingredients:

- 1 mug of oatmeal
- 1 egg
- 1 tablespoon of butter or margarine
- Salt and pepper to taste
- Optional: shredded cheese, diced onion, chopped green peppers

Instructions:

1. Preheat a nonstick skillet over medium heat.

2. Add the oatmeal and stir well to combine.

3. In a separate bowl, whisk together the egg and butter or margarine until smooth.

4. Add the egg mixture to the oatmeal mixture, and stir until everything is evenly combined.

5. Season with salt and pepper, if desired.

6. Cook for about 3 minutes, or until the eggs are set but still soft.

7. Serve hot with shredded cheese, diced onion, and chopped green peppers, if desired.

APPS AND SNACKS

Ingredients:

- 1 cup old-fashioned oats
- 1/4 cup chopped almonds
- 1/4 cup raisins
- 1/4 teaspoon ground cinnamon

Instructions:

1. Preheat oven to 350 degrees F (175 degrees C). Grease a baking sheet.

2. In a medium bowl, combine oats, almonds, raisins, and cinnamon.

3. Spread mixture on the baking sheet and bake for 10 minutes, or until lightly browned.

COCONUT SHRIMP

Ingredients:

- 1/2 pound large shrimp, peeled and deveined
- 1/4 cup chopped fresh cilantro
- 1/4 cup chopped fresh ginger
- 3 tablespoons soy sauce
- 1 tablespoon honey
- 1 teaspoon Sriracha sauce
- 1/4 teaspoon ground coriander

- 1/8 teaspoon ground cardamom
- 1/8 teaspoon ground cloves

Directions:

1. In a large bowl, combine the shrimp, cilantro, ginger, soy sauce, honey, Sriracha sauce, coriander, cardamom and cloves.
2. Mix well. Sprinkle with salt and pepper to taste.
3. Serve immediately or refrigerate for 30 minutes.

BUFFALO CHICKEN TOUCHES

Ingredients:

- 1 pound chicken breasts, pounded thin
- 1/2 cup Frank's Red Hot Buffalo Sauce
- 1/4 cup celery, diced
- 1/4 cup carrots, diced
- 1/4 cup red pepper flakes
- 1/4 cup white onion, diced
- 1 tablespoon olive oil

Instructions:

1. Preheat oven to 425 degrees.

2. In a large bowl, combine chicken, buffalo sauce, celery, carrots, red pepper flakes and white onion. Mix well.

3. Heat olive oil in a large skillet over medium heat. Add chicken mixture and cook for about 5 minutes per side or until cooked through. Serve hot!

TAQUITOS

Ingredients:

- 1 can black beans, drained and rinsed
- 1/2 cup cilantro, chopped
- 1/4 cup sour cream
- 6-8 corn tortillas
- 1 teaspoon chili powder
- 1 teaspoon garlic powder
- Salt, to taste

Instructions:

1. Preheat oven to 350 degrees.

2. In a bowl, combine black beans, cilantro, sour cream, corn tortillas and seasonings.

3. Place mixture into a greased 9x13 inch baking dish.

4. Bake for 25 minutes or until heated through.

THE FIERY GOAT

Ingredients:

- 1 goat
- 1 onion
- 1 tablespoon olive oil
- 1 red pepper
- 1 green pepper
- 3 cloves garlic, minced
- 2 tablespoons tomato paste
- 2 cups chicken broth
- 1 teaspoon cumin

- 1 teaspoon chili powder
- 1/2 teaspoon smoked paprika
- Sea salt and freshly ground black pepper, to taste

Instructions:

1. Heat the oil in a large pot over medium heat. Add the onions and peppers and cook until softened, about 5 minutes.
2. Add the garlic and cook for 1 minute more. Stir in the tomato paste and cook for 1 minute.
3. Add the goat, chicken broth, cumin, chili powder, smoked paprika, salt and pepper.
4. Bring to a boil then reduce the heat and simmer for 30 minutes.

SALADS

MASON JAR DRESSINGS

Ingredients:

- 1 cup olive oil
- 3 tablespoons red wine vinegar
- 2 tablespoons Dijon mustard
- 1 tablespoon honey
- 1 teaspoon dried oregano
- Kosher salt and freshly ground black pepper, to taste

Instructions:

1. In a small bowl, whisk together the olive oil, red wine vinegar, Dijon mustard, honey, oregano, salt and pepper.

2. Pour the dressing into a Mason jar.

3. Store in the fridge for up to 3 days.

SALAD BAR SALAD

Ingredients:

- 1 head of romaine lettuce, chopped
- 1 cup grape tomatoes, halved
- 1/2 cup red onion, diced
- 1/4 cup crumbled feta cheese
- 1/4 cup olives, pitted and sliced
- 1/4 cup vinaigrette dressing
- 1 tbsp. balsamic vinegar

Instructions:

1. In a large salad bowl, combine the romaine lettuce, grape tomatoes, red onion and feta cheese.

2. Drizzle with the vinaigrette dressing and toss to combine.

3. Sprinkle with olives and balsamic vinegar and serve chilled or at room temperature.

ROASTED GREEK SALAD

Ingredients:

- 3 cups of diced tomatoes
- 1/2 cup of diced onion
- 1/4 cup of diced red pepper
- 3 cloves of minced garlic
- 1 tsp. dried oregano
- 1/2 tsp. dried thyme
- Salt and pepper to taste
- 1/4 cup of olive oil
- 1/2 cup of white balsamic vinegar
- 1/4 cup of red wine vinegar
- 1 tbsp. sugar

Instructions:

1. Preheat oven to 375 degrees F (190 degrees C).
2. In a large bowl, mix together the diced tomatoes, onion, red pepper, garlic, oregano, thyme, salt and pepper.
3. Drizzle with the olive oil and mix well. Mix in the white balsamic vinegar, red wine vinegar and sugar.
4. Spread mixture into a baking dish and bake for 25 minutes or until bubbly.
5. Let cool slightly before serving

SHEET PAN SALAD

Ingredients:

- 1 head of romaine lettuce, chopped
- 1 red onion, diced
- 1 red bell pepper, diced
- 1 orange bell pepper, diced
- 1 cup crumbled feta cheese
- 2 tablespoons balsamic vinegar
- 2 tablespoons olive oil
- sea salt and black pepper to taste

Instructions:

1. Preheat the oven to 350 degrees F.

2. Spread out a single layer on a baking sheet and roast for about 20 minutes or until the lettuce is crispy and the onions are soft.

3. In a large bowl, combine the roasted vegetables, feta cheese, balsamic vinegar, olive oil, salt and pepper.

4. Serve immediately or store in an airtight container in the fridge for later.

BIG FESTIVE SALAD

Ingredients:

- 1 head of romaine lettuce, chopped
- 1/2 cup diced red onion
- 1/2 cup diced celery
- 1/2 cup diced green bell pepper
- 1/2 cup diced red grapes
- 1/4 cup diced black olives
- 3 tablespoons olive oil, divided
- 1 (12 ounce) can chickpeas, drained and rinsed
- 3 tablespoons balsamic vinegar
- 1 tablespoon Dijon mustard
- Sea salt and black pepper to taste

Instructions:

1. In a large salad bowl, combine romaine lettuce, red onion, celery, green bell pepper, red grapes, black olives, 1 tablespoon olive oil, chickpeas, balsamic vinegar, Dijon mustard, sea salt and black pepper.
2. Toss to combine. Serve chilled or at room temperature.

ARTY BREAD

Ingredients:

- 1 cup of all-purpose flour
- 1/2 teaspoon of salt
- 3 tablespoons of olive oil
- 1/4 cup of water
- 1 tablespoon of yeast

Instructions:

1) Preheat the oven to 350 degrees Fahrenheit.

2) In a bowl, mix the flour and salt together.

3) In a separate bowl, mix the olive oil and water together until they are combined.

4) Add the yeast to the wet ingredients and stir until it is dissolved.

5) Add the dry ingredients to the wet ingredients and stir until everything is combined.

6) Turn out the dough onto a lightly floured surface and knead for about 10 minutes.

7) Place the dough in a greased bowl and let it sit in a warm place for about an hour or until it has doubled in size.

8) Cut the dough into 12 pieces and shape them into rolls. Place them on a greased baking sheet and let them rise for about 20 minutes or until they have doubled in size again.

9) Bake for 25 minutes or until they are golden brown.

ITALIAN CHOPPED SALAD

Ingredients:

- 1/2 red onion
- 1/2 red bell pepper
- 1/4 cup chopped fresh parsley
- 1/4 cup chopped fresh basil
- 1/4 cup chopped fresh oregano
- 1 tablespoons olive oil
- 3 tablespoons balsamic vinegar
- 1 teaspoon Dijon mustard
- Kosher salt and black pepper to taste

Instructions:

1. In a large bowl, combine the onion, bell pepper, parsley, basil, oregano, oil, vinegar and mustard. Season with salt and black pepper to taste.
2. Toss to combine. Serve chilled or at room temperature.

MARKET BASKET SALAD

Ingredients:

- 1 large head of romaine lettuce
- 1/2 red onion, diced
- 1 tomato, diced
- 1/4 cup crumbled feta cheese
- 1/4 cup chopped fresh parsley
- 1/4 cup chopped fresh basil
- 2 tablespoons olive oil
- salt and pepper to taste

Instructions:

1. In a large salad bowl, combine the romaine lettuce, red onion, tomato, feta cheese, parsley, basil and olive oil.

2. Season with salt and pepper, to taste. Serve chilled or at room temperature.

SO-GOOD-FOR-YOU SALAD

Ingredients:

- 1 head of romaine lettuce
- 1/2 red onion, diced
- 1/2 cup diced celery
- 1/4 cup diced red pepper
- 6 tbsp. olive oil
- 1 tbsp. balsamic vinegar
- 1 tsp. Dijon mustard
- kosher salt and fresh cracked black pepper to taste

Instructions:

1) In a large bowl, combine the romaine lettuce, red onion, celery, and red pepper.

2) In a small bowl, whisk together the olive oil, balsamic vinegar, Dijon mustard, salt and black pepper to taste. Pour over the salad and toss to combine.

3) Serve chilled or at room temperature.

SOUPS AND STEWS

Ingredients:

- 1 onion, chopped
- 1 red pepper, chopped
- 1 bunch of celery, diced
- 1 carrot, peeled and diced
- 2 cloves garlic, minced
- 4 cups chicken or vegetable broth
- 1 can (14.5 ounces) diced tomatoes, undrained
- 1 teaspoon dried oregano
- 1/2 teaspoon salt
- Freshly ground black pepper to taste
- 1/2 cup uncooked white rice

Instructions:

1. In a large pot or Dutch oven, sauté the onion, red pepper, celery and carrot in olive oil until softened.
2. Add the garlic and sauté for an additional minute. Add the broth, tomatoes with their juice and oregano.
3. Bring to a boil then reduce heat and simmer for 30 minutes. Season with salt and black pepper to taste.

4. Stir in the rice and simmer for an additional 10 minutes.

11-CAN SOUP

Ingredients:

- 11 cans of soup (any variety)
- 1 cup of uncooked white rice
- 1 can of beef broth
- 1 can of tomato sauce
- 1 can of kidney beans
- 1 can of black beans
- 1 can of corn
- 1 teaspoon salt
- 1/2 teaspoon black pepper

Instructions:

1. Preheat oven to 375 degrees.

2. Cook rice according to package instructions. Once done, set aside.

3. In a large pot, combine all Soup ingredients and bring to a boil. Lower to a simmer and cook for 10 minutes.

4. ladle soup into bowls and top with cooked rice. Serve hot!

SIDE: EASY CHEESY TOAST

Ingredients:

- 2 slices of bread
- 1/2 cup grated cheddar cheese
- 1/4 cup diced onion
- 1 tablespoon butter

Instructions:

1. Preheat the oven to 350°F.

2. Spread one slice of bread with grated cheddar cheese and diced onion.

3. Place the other slice of bread on top, pressing down firmly so that the cheese and onion are evenly distributed.

4. Melt butter in a small saucepan over medium heat. Once melted, pour over the toast and cook for about 2 minutes until the cheese is melted and bubbly.

5. Remove from the oven and enjoy!

SPEEDY DUMPLING SOUP

Ingredients:

- 1 onion, diced
- 1 leek, diced
- 1 carrot, diced
- 2 celery ribs, diced
- 1 teaspoon ground cumin
- 1 teaspoon smoked paprika
- 1 teaspoon dried oregano

- 8 cups chicken stock
- 1 (14.5 ounce) can diced tomatoes, undrained
- 1 (6 ounce) can tomato paste
- 3/4 cup all-purpose flour
- 3/4 cup cold water
- Sea salt and freshly ground black pepper to taste

Instructions:

1. In a large soup pot over medium heat, sauté onions, leek, carrot and celery in oil until softened. Stir in cumin, smoked paprika and oregano.
2. Add the chicken stock and tomatoes with their juice. Bring to a boil then reduce heat to low and simmer for 30 minutes.
3. In a small bowl whisk together flour and water until smooth. Add to soup pot and stir until well blended. Season with salt and pepper to taste. Serve hot.

CHEESY TOMATO SOUP

Ingredients:

- 1 can diced tomatoes
- 1 tablespoon olive oil
- 1 onion, diced
- 3 garlic cloves, minced
- 1 teaspoon dried oregano
- 1 teaspoon dried basil
- 1/2 teaspoon salt
- 1/4 teaspoon black pepper
- 4 cups chicken broth

- 6 cups heavy cream
- 8 ounces cheddar cheese, shredded (2 cups)

Instructions:

1. Heat the oil in a large pot over medium heat. Add the onion and garlic and cook until softened, about 5 minutes.

2. Add the tomatoes, oregano, basil, salt, and pepper and bring to a simmer.

3. Cook until the tomatoes are broken down and the soup is thickened, about 10 minutes.

4. Stir in the chicken broth and bring to a simmer again.

5. Simmer for 10 more minutes to allow the flavors to meld.

6. Remove from heat and let cool slightly before serving. Ladle into bowls and top with cheese.

WHITE CHICKEN CHILI

Ingredients:

- 1 pound boneless, skinless chicken breasts
- 1 can black beans, drained and rinsed
- 1 can diced tomatoes
- 1 can corn
- 1 teaspoon chili powder
- 1 teaspoon garlic powder
- 1/2 teaspoon salt
- 1/4 teaspoon black pepper

Instructions:

1. Preheat oven to 375 degrees F (190 degrees C). Grease a baking dish with cooking spray.

2. In a large bowl, mix together the black beans, tomatoes, corn, chili powder, garlic powder, salt and pepper. Add in the chicken and toss to coat. Spread the mixture into the prepared baking dish. Bake for 30 minutes, or until chicken is cooked through. Serve hot.

BRACCO-FLOWER SOUP

Ingredients:

- 1 onion, diced
- 3 cloves garlic, minced
- 1 carrot, diced
- 1 celery stalk, diced
- 1 yellow bell pepper, diced
- 1 cup white wine
- 4 cups vegetable broth
- 1 teaspoon dried thyme
- 1/2 teaspoon dried oregano
- Kosher salt and freshly ground black pepper, to taste
- 6 ounces bracco cheese, crumbled (about 2 cups)
- 1/2 cup sour cream

Instructions:

1. In a large pot over medium heat, add the onions, garlic, carrot, celery stalk and bell pepper.

2. Sweat the vegetables until they are soft, about 5 minutes. Add the wine and bring to a simmer.
3. Add the vegetable broth and bring to a simmer. Add the thyme and oregano. Season with salt and black pepper. Stir in the bracco cheese.
4. Simmer until the cheese is melted and the soup is warmed through.
5. Serve garnished with sour cream.

TUSCAN CHICKEN SOUP

Ingredients:

- 1 rotisserie chicken, shredded
- 1 onion, chopped
- 1 carrot, chopped
- 3 cloves garlic, minced
- 2 cups chicken broth
- 1 tablespoon olive oil
- 1 teaspoon dried oregano
- 1/2 teaspoon dried thyme
- Salt and pepper, to taste
- 8 ounces white wine
- 6 ounces tomato sauce
- 1/4 cup chopped fresh parsley leaves

Instructions:

1. In a large soup pot or Dutch oven, heat the oil over medium heat. Add the onion, carrot, garlic and chicken; cook until the vegetables are tender, about 5 minutes.

2. Add the broth, oregano and thyme; bring to a simmer. Season with salt and pepper.

3. Reduce the heat to low and let the soup simmer for 30 minutes.

4. Add the wine and tomato sauce; simmer for 10 more minutes. Stir in the parsley leaves before serving.

CREAMY MUSHROOM SOUP

Ingredients:

- 1 tablespoon olive oil
- 1 small onion, diced
- 3 cloves garlic, minced
- 1 teaspoon dried thyme
- 1/2 teaspoon dried basil
- 1/4 teaspoon salt
- 1/4 teaspoon black pepper
- 2 pounds white mushrooms, sliced
- 3 cups chicken broth
- 1 cup heavy cream
- 1/4 cup grated Parmesan cheese

Instructions:

1. Heat the oil in a large pot over medium heat. Add the onion and garlic and cook until softened, about 5 minutes.
2. Add the thyme, basil, salt, and pepper and cook for 1 minute longer. Add the mushrooms and cook until browned, about 8 minutes. Add the chicken broth and bring to a simmer.
3. Reduce the heat to low and let simmer for 10 minutes. Remove from heat and let cool slightly.

4. In a blender or food processor, blend the soup until smooth. Return to the pot and stir in the cream and Parmesan cheese.
5. Serve warm.

RAMEN SOUP WITH SAUCY SHRIMP

Ingredients:

- 1 can of black beans
- 1 can of corn
- 1 can of diced tomatoes
- 2 cups of chicken broth
- 1 tablespoon of chili powder
- 1 teaspoon of smoked paprika
- 1 teaspoon of garlic powder
- 1/2 teaspoon of salt
- 1/4 teaspoon of black pepper
- 1 pound of shrimp, peeled and deveined
- 2 tablespoons of olive oil
- 1 cup of chopped onion
- 2 tablespoons of chopped celery
- 1 red bell pepper, cut into thin strips
- 3 cloves of garlic, minced

Instructions:

1. Preheat oven to 375 degrees Fahrenheit.

2. In a large pot or dutch oven, heat olive oil over medium heat. Add onion, celery, bell pepper and garlic; sauté for 5 minutes. Add in the black beans, corn, diced tomatoes and chicken broth. Bring to a boil. Reduce heat to low and simmer for 30 minutes.

Season with chili powder, smoked paprika, garlic powder and salt and pepper to taste.

3. Add shrimp to soup; cook for 3 minutes or until shrimp are pink and cooked through. Serve hot.

WHITE LASAGNA SOUP

Ingredients:

- 1 lb ground beef
- 1 onion, chopped
- 3 cloves garlic, minced
- 1 can diced tomatoes (14.5 oz)
- 1 can black beans (15 oz), rinsed and drained
- 1 can corn (13.25 oz), rinsed and drained
- 1 tsp chili powder
- 1 tsp cumin
- 1/2 tsp salt
- 8 cups chicken broth
- 8 lasagna noodles, cooked and cooled
- 1 (14 oz) can diced tomatoes with green chilies, undrained
- 1/4 cup chopped fresh cilantro leaves
- Extra virgin olive oil, for drizzling

Instructions:

1. In a large soup pot over medium heat, cook the ground beef until browned. Add the onion and garlic and cook until softened.
2. Add the tomatoes with their juices, black beans, corn, chili powder, cumin and salt. Stir in the chicken broth and bring to a boil.

3. Reduce the heat to low and simmer for 30 minutes.Meanwhile, prepare lasagna noodles according to package directions.
4. Just before serving, ladle the soup into bowls and top with lasagna noodles and diced tomatoes with green chilies.
5. Drizzle with extra virgin olive oil

PIZZA AND SANDWICHES

Ingredients:

- One pizza dough
- Mozzarella cheese
- Parsley
- Garlic
- Extra-virgin olive oil
- Onion
- Tomato sauce
- Salt and pepper to taste
- Pizza toppings of choice (e.g. pepperoni, mushroom, sausage, etc.)

Instructions:

1. Preheat your oven to 375 degrees F (190 degrees C).

2. On a lightly floured surface, roll out the pizza dough to a thin and even sheet.

3. Place the dough on a greased baking sheet and spread tomato sauce over the top.

4. Sprinkle mozzarella cheese over the sauce and then sprinkle parsley and garlic on top.

5. Top with your desired pizza toppings and bake in the preheated oven for about 20 minutes until the crust is golden brown and cheese is melted. Serve hot!

BROCCOLI-CHEESE STROMBOLI

Ingredients:

- 1 head broccoli
- 1 package shredded mozzarella cheese
- 1 jar spaghetti sauce
- 1 baguette
- Olive oil
- Salt and pepper to taste

Instructions:

1. Preheat oven to 350 degrees F (175 degrees C).

2. Cut broccoli into florets, discarding the stems.

3. In a large bowl, combine cheese, spaghetti sauce, and salt and pepper to taste.

4. Put broccoli florets in the mixture, making sure they are well coated.

5. Place the stromboli on a baking sheet and bake for about 20 minutes or until the cheese is melted and bubbly.

6. Slice the baguette and serve with the stromboli on top.

CLASSIC STROMBOLI

Ingredients:

- 1/2 pound broccoli florets
- 8 ounces mozzarella cheese, shredded
- 1/2 cup marinara sauce
- 1/4 cup grated Parmesan cheese
- 1/4 teaspoon garlic powder
- 1 large egg
- 1/4 teaspoon salt
- 1/4 teaspoon black pepper
- 1/4 sheet refrigerated pizza dough (14 inches)
- 1 tablespoon olive oil
- 1 small onion, chopped

Directions:

1. Preheat oven to 375 degrees F (190 degrees C). Grease a baking sheet.
2. In a large bowl, combine broccoli, mozzarella cheese, marinara sauce, Parmesan cheese, garlic powder, egg, salt and pepper.
3. Place the dough on a lightly floured surface; roll to a 12x18 inch rectangle. Spread the broccoli mixture over the dough. Sprinkle with onion.
4. Starting at one long end of the rectangle, roll up jellyroll fashion. Cut into twelve 1 1/2 inch slices. Place on prepared baking sheet.
5. Bake for 20 minutes or until crust is golden brown.

STEAK SANDWICH (OR SALAD!) BOARD

Ingredients:

- 1 flank steak
- 1 slice of bread
- 1 tomato, sliced
- 1 piece of cheese
- lettuce
- mayonnaise
- salt and pepper to taste

Instructions:

1. Preheat your grill to medium-high heat.

2. Season your steak with salt and pepper and grill for about 8 minutes per side, or until it reaches your desired doneness.

3. Toast your bread and spread with mayonnaise.

4. Layer the steak, tomato, cheese, and lettuce on top of the toasted bread.

5. Serve immediately!

PANTRY PIZZA PRONTO

Ingredients:

- 1/2 batch of pizza dough
- 1 jar marinara sauce
- 1/4 cup grated cheese
- 1/4 cup chopped pepperoni
- 1/4 cup chopped olives

Instructions:

1. Preheat oven to 475 degrees F. Roll out the dough on a lightly floured surface and place in a greased pizza pan.
2. Spread the sauce over the dough, then sprinkle with the cheese, pepperoni, and olives.
3. Bake for 10 minutes or until the crust is golden brown.

PEACH AND PROSCIUTTO FLATBREAD

Ingredients:

- 1/2 loaf of bread
- 1/4 cup of olive oil
- 1/4 cup of balsamic vinegar
- 1/2 teaspoon of salt
- 1/4 teaspoon of black pepper
- 1 large peach, thinly sliced
- 8 ounces prosciutto, thinly sliced

Instructions:

1. Preheat oven to 400 degrees F. Slice bread into 1" pieces and spread on a baking sheet.

2. Drizzle with olive oil and vinegar. Sprinkle with salt and pepper. Top with peach slices and prosciutto slices.
3. Bake for 15 minutes or until bread is golden brown.

AFFLUENCES

Ingredients:

- 1 cup water
- 1/4 cup white vinegar
- 1/4 teaspoon black pepper
- 1/4 teaspoon garlic powder
- 1/4 teaspoon onion powder
- 1 tablespoon olive oil
- 1 pound flank steak, thinly sliced against the grain

Instructions:

1. In a small bowl, whisk together water, vinegar, black pepper, garlic powder, and onion powder.
2. Pour mixture into a spray bottle and mist the steak with the mixture.
3. Heat olive oil in a large skillet over medium-high heat. Add the steak and cook for 3 to 4 minutes per side or until browned and cooked through.
4. Serve immediately.

FOUR SEASONS PIZZA

Ingredients:

- One baguette
- One jar of pizza sauce
- One can of crushed tomatoes
- One cup of shredded mozzarella cheese
- One cup of fresh basil leaves
- Salt and pepper to taste

Instructions:

1. Preheat oven to 375 degrees. Cut the baguette into four equal pieces.
2. Spread pizza sauce on each piece of bread. Top with crushed tomatoes, mozzarella cheese, and basil leaves.
3. Season with salt and pepper, then bake for about 20 minutes or until cheese is melted and bubbly.
4. Enjoy!

BARBECUE CHICKEN PIZZA

Ingredients:

- 1 pizza crust
- 1/2 cup barbecue sauce
- 1/4 cup brown sugar
- 1/4 cup ketchup
- 1 tablespoon Worcestershire sauce
- 1 teaspoon onion powder
- 1/4 teaspoon garlic powder
- 1/4 teaspoon black pepper
- 1 pound chicken breast, cooked and shredded
- 1 cup coleslaw mix or shredded cabbage

- 2 tablespoons diced red onion
- 2 tablespoons diced green bell pepper
- 2 tablespoons diced yellow bell pepper
- 1 tablespoon minced fresh cilantro

Instructions:

1. Preheat oven to 350 degrees F (175 degrees C). Place pizza crust on baking sheet.
2. In small bowl, combine barbecue sauce, brown sugar, ketchup, Worcestershire sauce, onion powder, garlic powder and black pepper; spread over crust.
3. Sprinkle chicken over sauce. Sprinkle coleslaw mix over chicken. Bake for 25 minutes.
4. Sprinkle with cilantro and serve.

CHEESEBURGER PIZZA

Ingredients:

- 1 pizza crust
- 1 lb. ground beef
- 1/2 cup ketchup
- 1/4 cup yellow mustard
- 1/4 cup brown sugar
- 1 tablespoon garlic powder
- 1 teaspoon onion powder
- 1/2 teaspoon salt
- 1/4 teaspoon black pepper
- 8 oz. cheese (cheddar, cheddar, blue cheese, etc.)
- 6 slices tomato
- 6 leaves green onion

Instructions:

1. Preheat oven to 400 degrees F. Spread ketchup on pizza crust.
2. Top with ground beef, blue cheese, and green onion.
3. Bake for 15 minutes or until crust is golden brown.

PASTA AND GRAINS

Ingredients:

- 1 pound spaghetti
- 1/2 cup vegetable broth
- 1/4 cup chopped fresh parsley
- 1 teaspoon salt
- 1/4 teaspoon black pepper
- 1/4 cup grated Parmesan cheese
- 1 tablespoon olive oil

Instructions:

1. Cook the spaghetti according to package instructions. Drain and rinse with cold water.

2. In a large bowl, whisk together the vegetable broth, parsley, salt, and pepper.

3. Add the cooked spaghetti and Parmesan cheese to the bowl and toss to combine.

4. In a large skillet over medium heat, heat the oil until hot. Add the pasta mixture and toss to combine. Cook for 3 to 4 minutes, or until heated through.

TACO SHELLS AND CHEESE

Ingredients:

- Taco shells
- Shredded cheese
- Salsa
- Green onions
- Hot sauce

Instructions:

1. Preheat oven to 350 degrees Fahrenheit.

2. Place the taco shells onto a baking sheet.

3. Top with shredded cheese and salsa.

4. Top with green onions and hot sauce.

5. Bake in preheated oven for 15 minutes or until cheese is melted and bubbly.

SHEET PAN GNOCCHI

Ingredients:

- 1 lb. gnocchi
- 1 tbsp olive oil
- 1 onion, chopped
- 1 green bell pepper, chopped
- 2 cloves garlic, minced
- 1/2 tsp. salt
- 1/4 tsp. black pepper
- 1 (14 oz) can diced tomatoes, undrained
- 1/4 cup chopped fresh parsley

- 6 tbsp. grated Parmesan cheese

Instructions:

1. Preheat oven to 375 degrees F (190 degrees C).

2. In a large bowl, combine gnocchi, olive oil, onion, bell pepper, garlic, salt and black pepper. Mix well and set aside.

3. Spread a layer of tomato sauce in the bottom of a large baking dish.

4. Add half of the gnocchi mixture to the dish and spread evenly. Top with another layer of sauce and then sprinkle with parsley and Parmesan cheese. Repeat the layers of gnocchi mixture and sauce until all is used up.

5. Bake for 25 minutes or until heated through and bubbly.

THE BEST FETTUCCINE ALFREDO

Ingredients:

- 1 lb. fettuccine
- 1/2 cup Alfredo sauce
- 1/4 cup grated Parmesan cheese
- 1 tablespoon chopped parsley
- Pinch of salt
- Freshly ground black pepper
- Extra-virgin olive oil for cooking

Instructions:

1. Cook the pasta in a large pot of salted water according to package instructions.

2. Meanwhile, heat the Alfredo sauce in a small saucepan over medium heat.

3. Drain the pasta and return it to the pot. Add the Alfredo sauce, Parmesan cheese, parsley, salt, and pepper to taste. Toss to combine, then divide the mixture among four plates.

4. Heat a large skillet over medium heat and add enough oil to coat the bottom. Add the pasta and cook, stirring occasionally, until heated through and slightly golden brown on the outside, about 8 minutes. Serve immediately.

ONE-POT SAUSAGE PASTA

Ingredients:

- 1 pound ground sausage
- 1 cup uncooked spaghetti
- 1/2 cup chopped onion
- 1/4 cup olive oil
- 1 (14.5 ounce) can diced tomatoes, undrained
- 1 tablespoon tomato paste
- 1 teaspoon sugar
- 1/2 teaspoon salt
- 1/4 teaspoon black pepper
- 10 ounces frozen chopped spinach, thawed and squeezed of excess water

Instructions:

1. In a large skillet over medium heat, cook the sausage until no longer pink; drain.

2. Add the spaghetti and onion to the skillet; cook and stir for 5 minutes or until the spaghetti is evenly coated with the sausage.

3. Add the oil and continue cooking for 5 minutes or until the spaghetti is tender.

4. Stir in the tomatoes, tomato paste, sugar, salt, and pepper. Bring to a boil; reduce heat and simmer for 10 minutes or until heated through.

5. Stir in the spinach and cook for 2 minutes or until wilted.

SHEET PAN MAC AND CHEESE

Ingredients:

- 1 lb. elbow macaroni
- 1/2 cup shredded cheddar cheese
- 1/4 cup all-purpose flour
- 1/4 teaspoon salt
- 1 tablespoon olive oil
- 1/2 cup milk
- 1 teaspoon paprika
- 1/4 teaspoon cayenne pepper
- Pinch of nutmeg

Instructions:

1. Preheat oven to 375 degrees F (190 degrees C).

2. Cook pasta according to package directions; drain.

3. In a small bowl, whisk together flour and salt; set aside.

4. Heat olive oil in a large saucepan over medium heat.

5. Add onion and cook until softened, about 5 minutes.

6. Stir in garlic and cook for 1 minute longer.

7. Add macaroni and saucepan mixture to a large baking dish; spoon flour mixture over top.

8. Bake for 20 minutes or until thickened and bubbly.

9. Stir in cheese and milk; heat until cheese is melted.

10. Season with paprika, cayenne, and nutmeg; serve hot.

HAWAIIAN SHRIMP BOWLS

Ingredients:

- 1 lb. shrimp, peeled and deveined
- 1/2 red onion, diced
- 1 red bell pepper, diced
- 2 tablespoons soy sauce
- 1 tablespoon rice vinegar
- 1 teaspoon honey
- 1 clove garlic, minced
- 1/4 teaspoon sesame oil
- 1/4 teaspoon ground ginger

Instructions:

1. In a large bowl, combine the shrimp, onion, bell pepper, soy sauce, rice vinegar, honey, garlic, sesame oil and ginger.
2. Toss to combine. Serve immediately.

BAKED RISOTTO

Ingredients:

- 1 tablespoon olive oil
- 1 onion, diced
- 3 cloves garlic, minced
- 1 pound Arborio rice
- 1 cup white wine
- 2 cups chicken broth
- Salt and pepper to taste

Instructions:

1. Preheat oven to 375 degrees F.

2. In a large skillet over medium heat, heat olive oil. Add onions and garlic and sauté for 5 minutes until softened.

3. Add rice and stir until coated with the onions and garlic. Sauté for 1 minute more.

4. Pour in white wine and let simmer for 2 minutes.

5. Stir in chicken broth and bring to a boil over high heat. Reduce heat to low, cover, and simmer for 20 minutes until all the liquid is absorbed. Season with salt and pepper to taste before serving.

BROCCOLI-CHEESE ORZO TO

Ingredients:

- 1 cup uncooked orzo
- 1/2 cup broccoli florets
- 1/4 cup shredded cheddar cheese
- 1 teaspoon olive oil
- Salt and pepper, to taste

Instructions:

1. Cook the orzo according to package instructions.

2. In a large skillet, heat the olive oil over medium heat. Add the broccoli and cook for 3 to 5 minutes, until tender.

3. Add the orzo and cheese to the skillet and stir well to combine. Season with salt and pepper, to taste. Serve hot!

VERY GREEN OROTON

Ingredients:

- 1/2 cup fresh cilantro leaves
- 1/2 lime
- 1/4 teaspoon kosher salt
- 1/4 teaspoon freshly ground black pepper
- 1/4 cup olive oil
- 1 small jalapeño pepper, seeded and finely chopped

Directions:

1. In a small bowl, whisk together the cilantro, lime juice, salt, and pepper.

2. In a medium bowl, whisk together the olive oil and jalapeño pepper. Pour the cilantro mixture into the bowl with the oil and stir to combine.

RAVIOLI ALLAY BETSY

Ingredients:

- 1 pound ravioli
- 1/2 cup Alfredo sauce
- 1/4 cup grated Parmesan cheese

Instructions:

1. Cook ravioli according to package directions.

2. In a small saucepan, heat the Alfredo sauce over medium heat.

3. Drain ravioli and place in a bowl. Pour the Alfredo sauce over the ravioli and sprinkle with Parmesan cheese. Serve immediately.

EASY SKILLETS

Ingredients:

- 1 tablespoon olive oil
- 1 pound ground beef
- 1 onion, diced
- 3 cloves garlic, minced
- 1 can (14.5 ounces) diced tomatoes, undrained
- 1 teaspoon dried oregano
- 1 teaspoon dried basil
- Pinch of salt and pepper

Instructions:

1. Heat the oil in a large skillet over medium heat. Add the ground beef and onion, and cook until the beef is browned, about 5 minutes.

2. Add the garlic, tomatoes, oregano, basil, salt and pepper, and bring to a simmer. Cook for 10 minutes to allow the flavors to meld. Serve hot.

CHICKEN-FRIED STEAK FINGERS

Ingredients:

- 4 chicken-fried steak fingers
- butter
- salt
- pepper
- onion
- garlic
- canola oil
- lemon juice

Instructions:

1. Preheat a large skillet over medium heat and melt butter. Season chicken-fried steak fingers with salt, pepper, and onion powder. Add to the hot butter and cook until golden brown and cooked through, about 5 minutes per side.

2. Place chicken-fried steak fingers on a serving plate and top with lemon juice and garlic. Serve hot!

SIDE: AWESOME ROASTED TOMATOES

Ingredients:

- 5-6 large tomatoes, cut in half
- 1 tablespoon olive oil
- 1 teaspoon salt
- 1/2 teaspoon black pepper
- 1/4 cup chopped fresh parsley

Instructions:

1. Preheat oven to 375 degrees. Arrange tomatoes, cut side down, in a single layer on a baking sheet.
2. Drizzle with oil and sprinkle with salt and pepper. Roast for 25 minutes, until skins are blistered and tomatoes are slightly soft when squeezed.
3. Let cool slightly, then chop into bite-sized pieces. Stir in parsley before serving.

BEEF NOODLE SKILLET

Ingredients:

- 1 pound beef stew meat
- 1 can black beans, drained and rinsed
- 1 can corn, drained
- 1 red pepper, de-seeded and chopped
- 1 red onion, diced
- 2 cloves garlic, minced
- 1 teaspoon chili powder
- 1 teaspoon ground cumin
- Salt and pepper to taste

Instructions:

1. Preheat your oven to 350 degrees Fahrenheit.

2. In a large skillet over medium heat, add in the beef stew meat and cook until browned all over.

3. Add in the black beans, corn, red pepper, red onion, garlic, chili powder, cumin, salt and pepper.

4. Stir everything together and cook until everything is heated through.

5. Serve warm with some rice on the side for a complete meal!

STIR-FRY WITH SCALLOPS

Ingredients:

- 1 pound scallops
- 1/2 cup vegetable oil
- 1 red bell pepper, diced
- 1 green bell pepper, diced
- 1 onion, diced
- 3 cloves garlic, minced
- 1 tablespoon ginger, grated
- 1 teaspoon honey
- 1/2 teaspoon soy sauce
- 1/4 teaspoon ground black pepper

Instructions:

1. Heat the oil in a large skillet over medium heat. Add the scallops and cook for 2 to 3 minutes per side until browned.

2. Add the bell peppers and onions and continue cooking for 5 to 7 minutes until the vegetables are tender.

3. Stir in the garlic, ginger, honey, soy sauce and black pepper and cook for 1 minute longer. Serve hot.

SPEEDY PORK SCALOPPINE

Ingredients:

- 1¼ lbs. boneless pork loin, cut into 1-inch cubes
- 1 tbsp. olive oil
- 1 tbsp. garlic, minced
- 1/2 tsp. salt
- 1/4 tsp. black pepper
- 1/4 cup all-purpose flour
- 1 cup chicken broth
- 6 oz. sliced scallops
- 6 cherry tomatoes, quartered
- 1/2 bunch fresh parsley, chopped

Instructions:

1. In a large skillet or wok over medium heat, heat the oil and gently stir in the pork cubes. Cook until lightly browned on all sides and cooked through, about 8 minutes.

2. Stir in the garlic, salt and pepper, then add the flour and cook for 1 minute more to combine. Gradually add the chicken broth, stirring constantly until mixture thickens and boils.

3. Add the scallops and cherry tomatoes and bring to a simmer, then reduce heat to low and simmer for 3 minutes until seafood is cooked through. Stir in parsley before serving.

SIDE: LOADED CRASH HOTS

Ingredients:

- 1 lb. ground beef
- 1 can black beans, drained and rinsed
- 1 can corn, drained
- 1 red pepper, seeded and diced
- 2 tablespoons chili powder
- 1 teaspoon cumin
- 1 teaspoon garlic powder
- 1/2 teaspoon salt

Instructions:

1. In a large skillet over medium heat, cook the ground beef until browned. Drain any excess fat.
2. Add the black beans, corn, red pepper, chili powder, cumin, garlic powder and salt. Stir until everything is combined.
3. Cook for about 10 minutes or until everything is heated through. Serve hot with your favorite toppings.

PEPPERONI FRIED RICE

Ingredients:

- 1 cup frozen peas
- 1 onion, diced
- 1 green bell pepper, diced
- 2 cups cooked white rice
- 1 cup pepperoni, diced
- 3 tablespoons olive oil
- Salt and black pepper to taste

Instructions:

1. Cook the rice according to package instructions.

2. In a large skillet over medium heat, heat the oil and cook the onion and bell pepper until softened.

3. Add the cooked rice and stir well to combine.

4. Add the pepperoni and peas and stir well to combine.

5. Cook for 2 to 3 minutes until heated through and evenly coated with spices. Serve warm.

SALMON BURGERS

Ingredients:

- 1 pound salmon
- 1 large onion, diced
- 2 cloves garlic, minced
- 1 tablespoon olive oil
- 1 teaspoon salt
- 1/2 teaspoon black pepper
- 4 hamburger buns
- lettuce leaves
- tomato slices
- mayonnaise
- salsa

Instructions:

1. Preheat the oven to 400 degrees F.

2. In a large bowl, combine the salmon, onion, garlic, olive oil and salt and pepper. Mix well and form into four burgers.

3. Place the burgers on a baking sheet and bake for 20 minutes or until cooked through. (You can also grill the burgers over medium heat).

4. Meanwhile, prepare the toppings by combining the lettuce leaves, tomato slices and mayonnaise in a small bowl.

5. To assemble the burgers, place one burger on each bun and top with the lettuce mixture and tomato slices. Serve with salsa on the side if desired

STEAK PIZZAIOLA

Ingredients:

- 4-6 thin sliced flank steak
- 1/2 cup olive oil
- 1 large onion, diced
- 3 cloves garlic, minced
- 1 (28 oz) can crushed tomatoes
- 1/4 cup tomato paste
- 1 teaspoon dried oregano
- 1/4 teaspoon dried basil
- 1/4 teaspoon black pepper
- 10 inches pizza dough, defrosted

Directions:

1. Preheat oven to 400 degrees. Heat olive oil in a large skillet over medium heat.
2. Add onions and garlic and sauté until soft. Add the steak and cook until browned on both sides.
3. Drain any excess fat. Add the tomatoes, tomato paste, oregano, basil, and pepper and bring to a simmer.

4. Place the steak on the pizza dough, spreading it out evenly.
5. Bake for 20 minutes or until crust is golden brown and steak is cooked through.

CHICKEN WITH MUSTARD HERB SAUCE

Ingredients:

- 1 lb. chicken breasts, skinless
- 1 tbsp. olive oil
- 1/2 tsp. dried oregano
- 1/4 tsp. black pepper
- 1/4 cup white wine vinegar
- 1 tbsp. Dijon mustard
- 1 tbsp. honey
- 3 cloves garlic, minced
- Salt and freshly ground black pepper to taste

Instructions:

1. Preheat oven to 400 degrees F (200 degrees C).

2. Heat olive oil in a large skillet over medium heat. Add chicken and cook until browned on both sides, about 4 minutes per side.

3. Remove chicken from pan and set aside in a baking dish.

4. Add oregano, pepper and vinegar to pan; bring to a boil over high heat. Cook for 1 minute, stirring occasionally.

5. Return chicken to pan; spoon sauce over it and toss to coat. Bake for 20 minutes or until chicken is cooked through.

6. Remove from oven and let cool for 5 minutes before serving

SIDE: LEMON-GARLIC SPINACH

Ingredients:

- 1 bunch of spinach
- 1/2 lemon
- 1 clove garlic, minced
- salt and pepper to taste
- Instructions:
- 1.Wash the spinach in cold water and spin it dry.
- 2.Squeeze the lemon over the spinach and toss with the garlic.
- 3.Season with salt and pepper to taste, and serve.

BRUSCHETTA CHICKEN

Ingredients:

- 1 pound boneless, skinless chicken breast, thinly sliced
- 1/2 cup olive oil
- 1/4 cup balsamic vinegar
- 1/4 cup chopped fresh basil
- 1 tablespoon honey
- Kosher salt and freshly ground black pepper
- 8 ounces tomato paste
- 8 ounces mozzarella cheese, thinly sliced
- 8 slices Italian bread, toasted

Instructions:

1. Preheat oven to 350 degrees F.

2. In a large bowl, combine chicken, olive oil, balsamic vinegar, basil, honey and 1 teaspoon salt and 1/2 teaspoon pepper. Toss

to coat. Spread mixture in a single layer on a baking sheet and roast for 20 minutes or until cooked through.

3. Remove from oven and let cool slightly.

4. In a small saucepan over medium heat, cook tomato paste until melted. Add mozzarella cheese and continue cooking until melted and bubbly. (If mixture begins to stick to the pan, add a little more liquid.)

5. To assemble bruschetta, place one slice of toast on each plate. Top with chicken mixture, then remaining toast slices.

CHICKEN CURRY IN A HURRY

Ingredients:

- 1 pound chicken breast, cut into cubes
- 1 onion, chopped
- 1 teaspoon garam masala
- 1 teaspoon ground cumin
- 1/2 teaspoon ground coriander
- 1 tablespoon olive oil
- 2 cloves garlic, minced
- 1 can (14.5 ounces) diced tomatoes, undrained
- 3 tablespoons tomato paste
- 2 cups water
- Salt and pepper, to taste

Instructions:

1. In a large skillet over medium heat, heat the olive oil. Add the chicken and onion and cook until the chicken is browned and the onion is softened, about 5 minutes.

2. Add the garam masala, cumin, coriander, and garlic and cook for 1 additional minute. Stir in the diced tomatoes with their juice, tomato paste, water, salt and pepper.
3. Bring to a boil over high heat. Reduce the heat to low and simmer for 30 minutes.

LOVIN' FROM THE OVEN

Ingredients:

- 1 sheet of puff pastry
- 1 egg
- 1 tablespoon of milk
- 1 tablespoon of melted butter
- 1 teaspoon of sugar
- 1/4 teaspoon of cinnamon
- pinch of salt

Instructions:

1. Preheat oven to 375 degrees F (190 degrees C). line a baking sheet with parchment paper. Roll out puff pastry to a 1/8 inch thickness.
2. Cut out desired shapes and place on prepared baking sheet. Beat together egg, milk, melted butter, sugar, cinnamon and salt.
3. Brush over each pastry cutout. Bake in preheated oven for 15 minutes or until puffed and golden brown.
4. Enjoy!

CHEESY GREEN BEAN AND RICE CASSEROLE

Ingredients:

- 1 cup cooked white rice
- 1/2 green bell pepper, diced
- 1/4 cup chopped onion
- 1/4 cup chopped celery
- 1/4 cup grated cheddar cheese
- 1 can (14 ounces) diced tomatoes, undrained
- 1 teaspoon garlic powder
- 1/8 teaspoon black pepper
- 1/2 cup shredded mozzarella cheese

Instructions:

1. Preheat oven to 350 degrees F. Spray a 9x13 inch baking dish with cooking spray.
2. In a large bowl, combine cooked rice, green bell pepper, onion, celery, cheddar cheese, diced tomatoes and garlic powder and pepper.
3. Spread mixture in the baking dish. Bake for 25 minutes or until cheese is melted.
4. Top with mozzarella cheese and bake for 5 minutes or until cheese is melted.

SPINACH RAVIOLI BAKE

Ingredients:

- 1 pound spinach
- 1/2 cup ricotta cheese
- 1 egg
- 1/4 teaspoon salt
- 1/4 teaspoon black pepper
- 1/4 cup grated Parmesan cheese
- 1 envelope (3.4 ounces) frozen ravioli, thawed
- 1/2 cup reduced-fat milk
- 2 tablespoons olive oil
- 1/2 cup shredded mozzarella cheese

Instructions:

1. Preheat oven to 400 degrees F. Grease a 9x13 inch baking dish with cooking spray.
2. In a large bowl, combine spinach, ricotta cheese, egg, salt and black pepper. Mix well. Spread mixture in the baking dish. Cover with frozen ravioli.
3. Bake for 15 minutes or until heated through. Sprinkle with Parmesan cheese and mozzarella cheese.
4. Bake 5 minutes longer or until cheese is melted.

TERIYAKI CHICKEN SHEET PAN SUPPER

Ingredients:

- 4 boneless, skinless chicken breasts
- 1/2 teaspoon salt
- 1/4 teaspoon black pepper
- 1 tablespoon olive oil
- 1/2 cup teriyaki sauce
- 1/4 cup soy sauce
- 1/4 cup rice vinegar
- 1 tablespoon honey

Instructions:

1. Preheat oven to 400 degrees F.

2. Season chicken with salt and pepper. Heat olive oil in a large skillet over medium heat. Add chicken and cook for 3 to 4 minutes per side until browned and cooked through.

3. Transfer chicken to a baking dish, spreading teriyaki sauce over top. Bake in preheated oven for 10 to 12 minutes, or until heated through.

4. In a small bowl, combine soy sauce, rice vinegar, and honey; pour over chicken in the baking dish. Bake for an additional 5 minutes, or until heated through.

CHEESY KALE CASSEROLE

Ingredients:

- 1 pound kale, chopped
- 1/2 cup almond milk
- 1/4 cup shredded cheddar cheese
- 1/4 teaspoon garlic powder
- 1/4 teaspoon onion powder
- 1 tablespoon olive oil
- Salt and pepper, to taste

Instructions:

1. Preheat oven to 350 degrees F.

2. In a large bowl, combine kale, almond milk, cheddar cheese, garlic powder, onion powder, and olive oil. Season with salt and pepper, to taste.

3. Transfer mixture to an 8x8 baking dish and bake for 20 minutes or until kale is wilted and cheese is melted. Let cool before serving.

MEATBALL AND POLENTA CASSEROLE

Ingredients:

- 1 pound ground beef
- 1 large egg
- 1/2 cup grated Parmesan cheese
- 1/4 cup chopped fresh parsley
- 1 tablespoon minced garlic
- 1/2 teaspoon salt
- 1/2 teaspoon black pepper

- 3 cups cooked polenta
- 1 (15 ounce) can tomato sauce
- 1 (8 ounce) package sliced mushrooms, quartered
- 1/2 cup shredded mozzarella cheese

Instructions:

1. Preheat oven to 350 degrees F. Grease a 9x13 inch baking dish. In a large bowl, mix together ground beef, egg, Parmesan cheese, parsley, garlic, salt and pepper. Shape mixture into 1 inch balls.
2. Place balls in the prepared baking dish. Bake for 20 minutes or until meatballs are browned and the cheese is melted. Meanwhile, in a small saucepan over medium heat, bring tomato sauce to a boil.
3. Add mushrooms and mozzarella cheese; cook for 5 minutes or until cheese is melted. Pour mushroom sauce over meatballs in the baking dish.
4. Bake for 10 more minutes or until bubbly.

VEGGIE TOT PIE

Ingredients:

- 1 can black beans, drained and rinsed
- 1 can corn, drained
- 1 bell pepper, diced
- 1 green onion, chopped
- 1 red pepper, diced
- 2 tablespoons olive oil
- 1 tablespoon chili powder
- 1 teaspoon cumin
- 1/2 teaspoon salt
- 1/4 teaspoon black pepper

- 8 oz. frozen cornbread dough, thawed
- 3/4 cup salsa (homemade or store bought)
- 1/2 cup shredded cheddar cheese

Instructions:

1. Preheat oven to 350 degrees F.

2. In a large bowl, combine black beans, corn, bell pepper, green onion, red pepper and olive oil.

3. In a smaller bowl, whisk together chili powder, cumin and salt and add to the large bowl.

4. Stir in cornbread dough until just combined. Pour mixture into an 8x8 inch baking dish and spread evenly. (If mixture is too wet to spread easily, add 1–2 tablespoons of flour until desired consistency is achieved.)

5. Bake for 25 minutes or until golden brown and bubbly.

6. Remove from oven

SHEET PAN MEATLOAF

Ingredients:

- 1 lb. ground beef
- 1 bell pepper, diced
- 1 onion, diced
- 1 can diced tomatoes
- 1 tsp salt
- 1 tsp black pepper
- 1/2 cup bread crumbs
- 1 egg
- 3 Tbsp ketchup

Instructions:

1. Preheat oven to 350 degrees. In a bowl, mix together ground beef, bell pepper, onion, tomatoes, salt and pepper.
2. In another bowl, mix together bread crumbs and egg. Stir in ketchup until well combined. Mold mixture into a loaf shape on a greased sheet pan.
3. Bake for 25 minutes or until cooked through.

SIDE: GARLIC-PARMESAN ROASTED BROCCOLI

Ingredients:

- 1 head of broccoli, cut into florets
- 1/4 cup olive oil
- 1/4 cup grated Parmesan cheese
- 1 teaspoon garlic powder
- Kosher salt and black pepper to taste

Instructions:

1. Preheat oven to 375 degrees F (190 degrees C).
2. Toss the broccoli with the olive oil, Parmesan cheese, garlic powder, salt, and pepper.
3. Spread on a baking sheet and roast for 20 minutes, or until tender. Enjoy!

GENERAL TSO'S CHICKEN

Ingredients:

- 1lb boneless, skinless chicken breasts
- 1 teaspoon cornstarch
- 1/2 teaspoon salt
- 1/2 teaspoon black pepper
- 1 tablespoon vegetable oil
- 3/4 cup chicken broth
- 3 tablespoons soy sauce
- 1 tablespoon honey
- 1 tablespoon rice vinegar
- 1 clove garlic, minced
- 1 teaspoon ground ginger

Instructions:

1. Preheat oven to 375 degrees F (190 degrees C).

2. In a shallow dish, combine cornstarch and salt; season chicken with the mixture. In another shallow dish, heat vegetable oil over medium heat.

3. Add the chicken to the first dish, and cook for 3 minutes or until lightly browned. Transfer to a baking dish.

4. In a small bowl, whisk together chicken broth, soy sauce, honey, rice vinegar, garlic, and ginger; pour over the chicken. Bake for 25 minutes or until cooked through.

LOW-EFFORT LASAGNA

Ingredients:

- 1 package lasagna noodles
- 1 tomato, diced
- 1 red onion, diced
- 1 bell pepper, diced
- 1 cup Ricotta cheese
- 1/2 cup Pesto sauce
- 1/4 cup grated Parmesan cheese
- Salt and pepper to taste

Instructions:

1. Preheat oven to 375 degrees F.

2. Cook lasagna noodles according to package instructions.

3. In a large bowl, mix together tomatoes, red onion, bell pepper, Ricotta cheese, pesto sauce, Parmesan cheese and salt and pepper to taste.

4. Spread the mixture over a 13x9 inch baking dish and top with noodles.

5. Bake for 25 minutes or until the cheese is melted and bubbly.

MEATY LAZY CHILES RELLENOS

Ingredients:

- 4 large poblano peppers
- 1 pound ground beef
- 1/2 cup shredded cheddar cheese
- 1/4 cup chopped fresh cilantro
- 1/4 teaspoon garlic powder
- 1 tablespoon olive oil

Instructions:

1. Preheat oven to 350 degrees.

2. Cut each pepper in half and remove seeds.

3. In a large skillet over medium heat, cook ground beef until browned.

4. Add onions, garlic powder, and cilantro; simmer for 10 minutes.

5. Stuff each pepper with beef mixture, and drizzle with olive oil.

6. Bake for 25 minutes, or until peppers are soft and browned.

TERRIFIC TEX-MEX

Ingredients:

- 1 lb. ground beef
- 1 can black beans, drained and rinsed
- 1 can corn, drained and rinsed
- 1/2 cup chopped onion
- 1/2 cup chopped green pepper
- 1 tsp. chili powder
- 1 tsp. cumin
- Salt and pepper, to taste

Instructions:

1. Preheat oven to 350°F.

2. In a large skillet over medium heat, cook the ground beef until browned.

3. Add the black beans, corn, onion, green pepper, chili powder and cumin, salt and pepper, to taste. Mix well and cook for 5 minutes more.

4. Spread the mixture in a baking dish and bake for 20 minutes or until heated through. Enjoy!

BEST-OF-BOTH-WORLDS ENCHILADAS

Ingredients:

- 1 can black beans
- 1 can corn
- 1 red onion, diced
- 1 green bell pepper, diced
- 2 tablespoons chili powder
- 1 teaspoon ground cumin
- 8 ounces enchilada sauce
- 8 soft tortillas
- 1 cup shredded cheddar cheese
- 1 cup sour cream
- 1 tablespoon chopped fresh cilantro

Instructions:

1. Preheat oven to 375 degrees F (190 degrees C).

2. In a large bowl, combine black beans, corn, red onion, green bell pepper, chili powder, and ground cumin.

3. Spoon mixture into the center of each tortilla.

4. Roll up tortillas and place on a baking sheet.

5. Bake for 15 minutes or until heated through.

6. In a small saucepan over medium heat, heat enchilada sauce until hot.

7. Spoon enchiladas onto plates; top with cheese, sour cream, and cilantro.

CHORIZO BURGERS

Ingredients:

- 1 pound chorizo sausage
- 1 egg
- 1/2 cup panko bread crumbs
- 1 teaspoon garlic powder
- 1/2 teaspoon onion powder
- 1/4 teaspoon black pepper
- 1 tablespoon olive oil, divided
- 8 hamburger buns
- lettuce, tomato, red onion, avocado, mayonnaise or mustard, and salt and pepper to taste

Instructions:

1. Preheat your grill to medium high heat.

2. In a bowl, mix together the chorizo sausage, egg and panko bread crumbs.

3. Add in the garlic powder, onion powder and black pepper and mix until well combined.

4. Split the mixture into 8 equal portions and shape each into a ball.

5. Coat each ball in olive oil then place on the grill and cook for about 5 minutes per side until browned and cooked through.

6. Assemble your burgers by placing a spoonful of lettuce, tomato, red onion, avocado and mayonnaise on each bun then top with a grilled chorizo ball. Sprinkle with salt and pepper to taste and serve immediately!

SIDE: TACO TOTS

Ingredients:

- 1 package taco shells
- 1 can refried black beans
- 1/2 cup shredded cheddar cheese
- 1/4 cup diced tomatoes

Instructions:

1. Preheat the oven to 350 degrees F. Line a baking sheet with parchment paper and set aside.
2. In a medium bowl, mix together the black beans, cheddar cheese, and diced tomatoes.
3. Place the taco shells on the prepared baking sheet. Spoon the bean mixture evenly into each shell.
4. Bake for 10 minutes or until the shells are golden brown. Enjoy!

FISH STICK TACOS

Ingredients:

- 4-6 fish sticks
- 1/2 cup salsa
- 1/2 cup chicken or beef broth
- 1/4 cup chopped onion
- 1 tablespoon olive oil
- 8-10 small tacos shells

Instructions:

1. Preheat the oven to 400 degrees F.

2. In a baking dish, place the fish sticks in an even layer.

3. In a small bowl, mix together the salsa, chicken broth and chopped onion. Pour mixture over the fish sticks and bake for 20 minutes or until the fish sticks are cooked through.

4. In a large skillet, heat the olive oil over medium heat. Add the tacos shells and cook for about 5 minutes or until warmed through. Top with cooked fish sticks and salsa before serving.

SHEET PAN QUESADILLA

Ingredients:

- 8-12 oz. of boneless, skinless chicken breast
- 1/2 cup of all-purpose flour
- Salt and pepper, to taste
- 1/4 teaspoon of chili powder
- 1/4 teaspoon of cumin
- 2 tablespoons of olive oil
- 8 oz. of quesadilla cheese (cheddar, pepper jack, or any other flavor you like)
- 1/2 cup of salsa (homemade or storebought)

Instructions:

1. Preheat your oven to 350 degrees Fahrenheit.

2. Dust your chicken breast with flour, salt, and pepper, then grill it for about 5 minutes per side, until cooked through but still pink in the center.

3. In a large skillet over medium heat, heat up the olive oil until hot. Add the cooked chicken and sauté until browned on all sides.

4. Assemble your quesadilla by placing one piece of cheese on one half of the grilled chicken breast and topping it with salsa. Fold the other half over the top and serve immediately.

FESTIVE PORK CHOPS

Ingredients:

- 4 pork chops
- 1 teaspoon salt
- 1 teaspoon pepper
- 1 tablespoon olive oil
- 1 onion, chopped
- 3 cloves garlic, minced
- 1 cup apple cider vinegar
- 3 tablespoons honey
- 3 tablespoons Dijon mustard

Instructions:

1. Preheat oven to 400 degrees F. Season pork chops with salt and pepper. Heat olive oil in a large skillet over medium heat. Add the pork chops and cook for 3 minutes per side or until browned.

2. Transfer to a baking dish and bake for 10 minutes or until thermometer reads 145 degrees F.

3. In a small bowl, whisk together apple cider vinegar, honey, Dijon mustard. Pour over the pork chops and serve immediately.

SIDE: QUICK MEXICAN RICE

Ingredients:

- 1 cup uncooked white rice
- 1 can black beans, drained and rinsed
- 1/2 diced green bell pepper
- 1/4 diced red onion
- 1 tablespoon olive oil
- 1 teaspoon chili powder
- 1/2 teaspoon cumin

Instructions:

1. In a medium bowl, combine the rice, black beans, bell pepper, and onion.

2. Heat the oil in a large skillet over medium heat. Add the mixture and cook until the vegetables are tender, about 5 minutes.

3. Stir in the chili powder and cumin and cook for an additional minute. Serve hot.

HONEY-CHIPOTLE SALMON

Ingredients:

- 4-6 salmon fillets
- 1/4 cup honey
- 1 tbsp. olive oil
- 1 tsp. chili powder
- 1/4 tsp. smoked paprika
- 1/4 tsp. ground cumin
- sea salt and black pepper, to taste

- 2 tablespoons chopped fresh cilantro

Instructions:

1. Preheat oven to 400 degrees F (200 degrees C).
2. In a small bowl, whisk together honey, olive oil, chili powder, smoked paprika and cumin.
3. Season salmon with salt and black pepper and spread honey mixture over top of each fillet.
4. Place salmon on a baking sheet and bake for 10 minutes, or until fish is just cooked through.
5. Sprinkle with fresh cilantro before serving.

TAMALE PIE

Ingredients:

- 1 can black beans, drained and rinsed
- 1 can corn, drained and rinsed
- 1 red onion, diced
- 1 green bell pepper, diced
- 1 tablespoon chili powder
- 1 teaspoon cumin
- 1/2 teaspoon garlic powder
- 1/2 teaspoon smoked paprika
- 1/2 teaspoon salt
- 8 ounces tamale sauce (homemade or store bought)
- 6 cups cooked white rice
- 8 eggs, beaten
- 1 cup chopped cilantro

Instructions:

1. Preheat oven to 350 degrees. Grease a 9x13 inch baking dish. In a large bowl, mix together black beans, corn, red

onion, green bell pepper, chili powder, cumin, garlic powder, smoked paprika and salt.

2. Pour mixture into the prepared baking dish. Spread tamale sauce across the top of the mixture.
3. In a separate bowl, mix together eggs and cilantro. Pour egg mixture over tamale sauce.
4. Bake for 30 minutes or until set.

DESSERTS

SHORTCUT TRES LECHES CAKE

Ingredients:

- 1 can sweetened condensed milk
- 1 cup all-purpose flour
- 1/2 teaspoon baking powder
- 1/2 teaspoon baking soda
- pinch of salt
- 8 tablespoons (1 stick) unsalted butter, at room temperature
- 2 large eggs
- 1 cup whole milk
- 3 tablespoons sugar
- 1 tablespoon vanilla extract

Instructions:

1. Preheat oven to 350 degrees F (175 degrees C). Butter and flour a 9x13 inch baking pan.

2. In a medium bowl, whisk together the flour, baking powder, and baking soda. Set aside.

3. In another medium bowl, whisk together the condensed milk, milk, sugar, and vanilla extract.

4. Pour the wet ingredients into the dry ingredients and mix until just combined.

5. Pour the batter into the prepared pan and bake for 30 to 35 minutes, or until a toothpick inserted into the center comes out clean. Let cool before serving.

RUSTIC STRAWBERRY TART

Ingredients:

- 1 pre-made crust
- 1/2 cup sugar
- 1/4 teaspoon salt
- 3 tablespoons cornstarch
- 3 tablespoons cold butter, diced
- 1/2 cup sliced strawberries
- 1/4 teaspoon lemon juice
- 1 tablespoon flour
- 1 tablespoon sugar
- 1 tablespoon flour
- Pinch of salt

Instructions:

1. Preheat oven to 375 degrees F (190 degrees C).

2. In a small bowl, mix together 1/2 cup sugar, 1/4 teaspoon salt and 3 tablespoons cornstarch. Set aside.

3. In a large bowl, cream together 3 tablespoons cold butter and 1/2 cup sliced strawberries until light and fluffy. Add lemon juice and flour and mix until well combined. Pour mixture into crust.

4. In a small bowl, mix together 1 tablespoon sugar and 1 tablespoon flour. Sprinkle over strawberry mixture. Bake for 25 minutes or until set.

BROWNIE S'MORES BARS

Ingredients:

- 1/2 cup (120 ml) unsalted butter, at room temperature
- 1 cup (240 ml) granulated sugar
- 2 large eggs
- 1 teaspoon pure vanilla extract
- 1 1/2 cups all-purpose flour
- 1 teaspoon baking powder
- pinch of salt
- 8 ounces dark chocolate, chopped
- 1/2 cup milk chocolate chips

Instructions:

1. Preheat oven to 350 degrees F (175 degrees C). Butter an 8x8 inch baking dish.
2. In a medium bowl, using an electric mixer on medium speed, cream butter and sugar until light and fluffy.
3. Add eggs, one at a time, beating well after each addition. Stir in vanilla. In a small bowl, whisk together flour, baking powder and salt.
4. Gradually add to butter mixture just until blended. Stir in chocolate and milk chocolate chips.

5. Pour batter into the prepared dish. Bake for 25 to 30 minutes or until a wooden toothpick or cake tester inserted into the center comes out clean.
6. Let cool completely before cutting into bars.

ROOT BEER FLOAT PIE

Ingredients:

- 1 pie crust
- 1 cup root beer
- 1/2 cup heavy cream
- 1/4 teaspoon nutmeg
- 1/4 teaspoon allspice
- Pinch of salt
- Sweetener (optional)

Instructions:

1. Preheat oven to 425 degrees F (220 degrees C).

2. Pour root beer in a small saucepan and heat over medium heat until warmed.

3. In a medium bowl, whisk together heavy cream, nutmeg, allspice, and salt.

4. Pour warmed root beer mixture into the bowl with the cream and stir until combined. If desired, add a sweetener to taste.

5. Pour mixture into the pie crust and bake for 15 minutes, or until set. Serve warm.

GRILLED PINEAPPLE WITH CREAM

Ingredients:

- 1 pineapple
- 1 tbsp. olive oil
- 1/4 tsp. salt
- 1/4 tsp. black pepper
- 1 tbsp. white vinegar
- 1/4 cup heavy cream

Instructions:

1. Preheat grill to medium heat.

2. Cut pineapple into 1-inch thick slices.

3. In a small bowl, whisk together olive oil, salt, and pepper.

4. Rub the mixture all over the pineapple slices.

5. Place pineapple slices on the grill and cook for 3 minutes per side, or until grill marks appear.

6. Remove from grill and drizzle with white vinegar; serve immediately with heavy cream on the side for dipping

ICE CREAM LAYER CAKE

Ingredients:

- 1 cup all-purpose flour
- 1/2 teaspoon baking powder
- pinch of salt
- 1/2 cup (1 stick) unsalted butter, at room temperature
- 3/4 cup granulated sugar
- 3 large eggs, at room temperature
- 1/2 cup whole milk
- 1 teaspoon vanilla extract
- 1 quart ice cream, softened (optional)

Instructions:

1. Preheat oven to 350 degrees F. Butter and flour one 9x13 inch baking pan.
2. In a medium bowl, whisk together flour, baking powder and salt. With an electric mixer on medium speed, beat butter in a medium bowl until creamy.
3. Add granulated sugar and beat until light and fluffy. Beat in eggs one at a time, then add milk and vanilla extract. With the mixer on low speed, add the dry ingredients alternately with the ice cream until just blended.
4. Pour batter into prepared pan and spread evenly. Bake for 30 minutes or until a toothpick inserted into the center comes out clean.
5. Cool cake in pan for 10 minutes before transferring to a wire rack to cool completely.

PEACH-BASIL SHORTCAKES

Ingredients:

- 1 cup all-purpose flour
- 1/2 teaspoon baking powder
- pinch of salt
- 1/4 cup unsalted butter, at room temperature
- 1/2 cup granulated sugar
- 2 large eggs, beaten
- 1/3 cup peach jam or preserves
- 1 tablespoon chopped fresh basil leaves

Instructions:

1. Preheat oven to 425 degrees F (220 degrees C). Line a baking sheet with parchment paper.
2. In a medium bowl, whisk together flour, baking powder and salt.
3. In the bowl of an electric mixer fitted with the paddle attachment, beat butter on medium speed until creamy. Add granulated sugar and continue beating until mixture is light and fluffy.
4. Add eggs one at a time, mixing well after each addition. With mixer on low speed, add flour mixture alternately with peach jam or preserves. Stir in basil leaves.
5. Drop dough by rounded tablespoons onto prepared baking sheet.
6. Bake for 12 to 15 minutes, until shortcakes are golden brown and firm to the touch.

THE BEST CHOCOLATE POKE CAKE

Ingredients:

- 1 cup all-purpose flour
- 1/2 teaspoon baking powder
- pinch of salt
- 1/4 cup unsweetened cocoa powder
- 1/4 cup granulated sugar
- 1/4 cup light brown sugar, packed
- 3 large eggs, beaten
- 1/3 cup vegetable oil
- 2 teaspoons vanilla extract
- 1 1/2 cups semi sweet chocolate chips (or any other chocolate chips)

Instructions:

1. Preheat oven to 350 degrees F. Grease and flour an 8x8 inch baking pan. In a medium bowl, whisk together flour, baking powder and salt. Set aside.
2. In a small bowl, whisk together cocoa powder, sugars and eggs until well combined.
3. Add oil and vanilla extract and mix until smooth. Pour mixture into the prepared pan and bake for 25 minutes or until a toothpick inserted into the center comes out clean.
4. Sprinkle with chocolate chips before serving. Enjoy!

COCONUT CREAM PIE

Ingredients:

- 1 pie crust
- 1 cup of sugar
- 3 eggs
- 1/4 cup of flour
- 1/4 teaspoon of salt
- 1/2 cup of unsweetened coconut milk
- 1/4 cup of light corn syrup
- 1 teaspoon of vanilla extract
- 1/4 teaspoon of baking soda
- 8 ounces of cream cheese, softened
- 1 tablespoon of butter, melted

Instructions:

1. Preheat oven to 350 degrees F. Grease a 9 inch pie dish. In a large bowl, whisk together the sugar, eggs, flour, and salt.
2. Add the coconut milk, corn syrup, and vanilla extract and mix until smooth. Pour the filling into the prepared pie dish.
3. Bake in the preheated oven for 10 minutes or until set. In a small bowl, mix together the cream cheese and butter until well blended.
4. Spread over the top of the pie and bake for an additional 10 minutes or until set.

TOP-SECRET CHOCOLATE CAKE

Ingredients:

- 1 3/4 cups all-purpose flour
- 1 1/2 teaspoons baking powder-pinch of salt
- 3/4 cup unsweetened cocoa powder
- 1 1/2 sticks (3/4 cup) unsalted butter, at room temperature
- 2 cups granulated sugar
- 2 large eggs, beaten
- 1 teaspoon vanilla extract
- 1 cup milk
- 1 tablespoon vinegar

Instructions:

1. Preheat oven to 350 degrees F (175 degrees C). Butter and flour one 9x13 inch baking pan. Sift together flour, baking powder, and salt; set aside.
2. In medium bowl with electric mixer on low speed, beat butter until creamy. Add granulated sugar and beat until light and fluffy. Beat in eggs one at a time, then stir in vanilla extract.
3. With mixer on low speed, add flour mixture alternately with milk to butter mixture in medium bowl until just blended. Pour batter into prepared pan.
4. Bake for 30 minutes or until cake springs back when lightly touched.
5. Cool cake in pan on wire rack for 10 minutes; turn out onto rack to cool completely.

CINNAMON APPLES

Ingredients:

- 6-8 cinnamon apples
- 1/4 cup brown sugar
- 1 teaspoon ground cinnamon
- pinch of salt

Instructions:

1. Preheat oven to 375 degrees F (190 degrees C).

2. Core the apples, then slice thin.

3. In a small bowl, whisk together brown sugar, cinnamon, and salt.

4. Place apple slices in a baking dish and top with sugar mixture.

5. Bake for 25 minutes, or until bubbly. Serve hot!

EASY "FRIED" ICE CREAM

Ingredients:

- 1 cup heavy cream
- 1/2 cup sugar
- 1 tsp vanilla extract
- 4 cups ice cream
- 1/2 cup all-purpose flour
- 1 tbsp salt
- 2 cups vegetable oil, for frying

Instructions:

1. In a medium bowl, stir together the heavy cream, sugar, and vanilla extract. Pour mixture into a deep fryer or large saucepan and heat over medium heat until hot but not boiling.

2. Add the ice cream and continue to cook, stirring frequently, until mixture thickens and coats the back of a spoon. Remove from heat and let cool slightly.

3. Stir in the flour and salt until well combined. Pour mixture into a shallow dish. Heat vegetable oil in a large skillet over medium heat until hot but not smoking. Scoop 1/4 cup of batter to form each piece of fried ice cream. Carefully place in hot oil and fry until golden brown, about 2 minutes per side. Drain on paper towels before serving.

BLACKBERRY ICEBOX CAKE

Ingredients:

- 1 cup all-purpose flour
- 1 teaspoon baking powder
- 1/2 teaspoon baking soda
- pinch of salt
- 6 tablespoons unsalted butter, at room temperature
- 1/2 cup granulated sugar
- 1 large egg, beaten
- 2 cups blackberries, fresh or frozen
- 1/4 cup honey
- 1 tablespoon bourbon whiskey (or any other strong liquor)

Instructions:

1. Preheat oven to 350 degrees F. Butter and flour one 9x13 inch baking pan. Set aside.

2. In a medium bowl, whisk together flour, baking powder and baking soda. Stir in salt. Set aside.

3. In the bowl of an electric mixer fitted with the paddle attachment, beat butter on medium speed until creamy. Add granulated sugar and continue beating until light and fluffy. Beat in egg until well combined. Add blackberry puree and honey and beat until well combined. Add flour mixture to wet ingredients and beat until just combined. Pour batter into prepared pan and spread evenly. Bake for 30 minutes or until a toothpick inserted into the center comes out clean. Cool cake in pan for 10 minutes before inverting onto a cutting board to remove from pan completely

THE BEST POTLUCK DESSERT EVER

Ingredients:

- 1 package of chocolate pudding mix
- 1 container of whipped cream
- 1 can of cherry pie filling

Instructions:

1. Preheat your oven to 350 degrees Fahrenheit.

2. Arrange a layer of chocolate pudding in the bottom of a 9×13 inch baking dish.

3. Top with a layer of whipped cream and spread evenly.

4. Spoon cherry pie filling over the whipped cream and spread evenly.

5. Repeat steps 2-4 until the dish is full.

6. Bake for 25 minutes, or until the pudding is set and the edges are lightly browned. Serve immediately!

MUG CAKES

Ingredients:

- 1 mug
- 1 egg
- 1/4 cup sugar
- 1 tablespoon butter
- flour for dusting
- pinch of salt
- coffee, to taste (optional)

Instructions:

1. Preheat oven to 350 degrees F (175 degrees C). Grease or line a mug with enough flour to coat. In a small bowl, whisk together the egg and sugar.
2. Pour the mixture into the prepared mug. Melt the butter in a small saucepan over low heat. Stir in the coffee until well combined.
3. Spoon the coffee mixture over the top of the batter in the mug. Bake for 15 minutes, or until golden brown and set.

ROASTED MISO NOODLES

Ingredients:

- 1 package of ramen noodles
- 1 tablespoon of miso paste
- 1 tablespoon of soy sauce
- 1 teaspoon of sesame oil
- 2 cloves of garlic, minced
- 1 cup of bean sprouts
- 1/4 cup of green onions, chopped

Instructions:

1. Preheat your oven to 400 degrees Fahrenheit.

2. Cook the ramen noodles according to the instructions on the package.

3. In a mixing bowl, mix together the miso paste, soy sauce, and sesame oil.

4. Pour the mixture into a baking dish and top with the cooked noodles, bean sprouts, and green onions. Bake for 15 minutes or until everything is hot and bubbly. Serve immediately!

SALAD FROM VIETNAM

Ingredients:

- 1 head of Napa or other salad cabbage
- 1/2 red onion, diced
- 1 fresh gingerroot, peeled and finely chopped
- 1 lime, juiced
- 1 tablespoon fish sauce
- 1 teaspoon sugar
- 1/4 teaspoon ground turmeric
- 1/4 teaspoon ground coriander
- 5 cups vegetable broth
- 6 small red Thai chilies, seeded and thinly sliced
- 10 large fresh mint leaves, shredded (about 2 cups)

Instructions:

1. In a large bowl, mix together the cabbage, onion, gingerroot, lime juice, fish sauce, sugar and turmeric.

2. Pour in the vegetable broth and adjust seasoning with salt and pepper to taste.

3. Mix in the Thai chilies and mint and serve chilled or at room temperature.

NOODLES CURRY SOUP

Ingredients:

- 1 can of coconut milk
- 1 onion, chopped
- 3 cloves of garlic, minced
- 1 teaspoon curry powder
- Salt and pepper to taste
- 1 package of ramen noodles
- 2 cups vegetable broth
- 1 cup frozen peas
- 1 carrot, peeled and chopped
- 1 bell pepper, seeded and chopped
- 1 tablespoon olive oil or butter
- Shredded cheddar cheese (optional)

Instructions:

1. In a large pot, heat the oil or butter over medium heat. Add the onion and garlic and cook until softened, about 5 minutes. Add the curry powder and salt and pepper to taste.
2. Add the ramen noodles and vegetable broth. Bring to a boil, then reduce the heat to low and simmer for 10 minutes. Add the peas and carrots and simmer for another 5 minutes.
3. Serve with shredded cheddar cheese if desired.

CREAMY NUTS AND NOODLES SALAD

Ingredients:

- 1/2 cup cooked white or brown rice
- 1/4 cup chopped fresh parsley
- 1/4 cup chopped fresh cilantro
- 2 tablespoons olive oil
- 1 teaspoon grated lemon zest
- 1/4 teaspoon ground cumin
- Salt and pepper, to taste
- 3/4 pound skinless, boneless chicken breasts, cut into bite-sized pieces
- 3 tablespoons soy sauce
- 1 tablespoon honey
- 1 tablespoon sesame oil
- 8 ounces wide egg noodles

Directions:

1. Cook the rice according to package instructions.

2. In a large bowl, combine the cooked rice, parsley, cilantro, olive oil, lemon zest and cumin. Season with salt and pepper, to taste.

3. Add the chicken and soy sauce to the bowl and toss to coat.

4. In a separate large skillet over medium heat, warm the honey and sesame oil until hot.

5. Add the egg noodles and toss to coat with the honey and sesame oil.

6. Divide the noodles among 4 plates and top with the chicken salad.

LUNCH BOX NOODLES

Ingredients:

- 1 package of ramen noodles
- 1 can of black beans
- 1/2 a red onion
- 1/2 a green bell pepper
- 1 tsp. chili powder
- 1 tsp. cumin
- sea salt and black pepper to taste
- shredded cheese (optional)

Instructions:

1. Cook the ramen noodles according to the instructions on the package.

2. While the noodles are cooking, heat up a large skillet over medium heat. Add in the black beans, red onion, bell pepper, chili powder, cumin, salt and black pepper. Cook for about 10 minutes until everything is cooked through.

3. Drain any excess liquid from the skillet, then mix in the ramen noodles and shredded cheese (if using). Serve warm!

.....The End.....

Printed in Great Britain
by Amazon